THE ADVENTURES OF HENRY DENT

Farmer, Poet, Gold Digger, Sawyer

Cathy Smith

authorHOUSE®

AuthorHouse™ UK Ltd.
500 Avebury Boulevard
Central Milton Keynes, MK9 2BE
www.authorhouse.co.uk
Phone: 08001974150

First published by AuthorHouse   10/7/2010

ISBN: 978-1-4520-8102-1 (sc)

This book is printed on acid-free paper.

A Sawyer's Hut on the River Huon by Wm Knight 1842

Introduction

"The First Aspirations of Thought written for Amusement and doomed to the flames."

These words were written by 20 year old Henry Dent of Bolton in Westmorland, in the year 1847 on the first page of a notebook in which he painstakingly wrote out poems of his own composing. Little did he know that only a few years later it would be he who perished in flames, whilst the notebook survived in an attic for over a hundred years.

Henry's death is commemorated by a tombstone stating that he died at Flight's Bay, Van Diemen's Land on January 11th 1854, aged 27 years, and was interred at Franklin. How did he come to die so far away from home? Thanks to members of his family, many of his letters home have been preserved, and from these we can piece together his short but adventurous life.

Henry was born and brought up in the small village of Bolton, which is four miles from Appleby, then the county town of Westmorland. It was a small rural community, with houses well spaced along north-south, and east-west axes, with the river Eden a little way to the east, below the 12th century Church. The hills of the Pennines are clearly visible to the east, with the Lake District fells more distant in the other direction. In 1811 there were 65 houses in the parish, and this grew slowly to around 80 by mid-century, the population then being around 380 persons. The striking fact when viewing the 1851 census is the number of children, around 145 under the age of 14. This coincides with the astounding doubling of the population of England from 10.5 to 21 million in the years between 1801 and 1851.

Henry was the second of eight children born to John and Agnes Dent of Gilflosh Farm (later known as Elm House), which is situated prominently in the village, next to the crossroads. The Dents, yeoman farmers, may have benefited from the enclosure of village common lands earlier in the century, as John Dent, along with a John Dixon, were already the largest land owners in 1828. In 1851 John Dent was listed as a farmer of 180 acres. This was the largest farm in the village proper, only surpassed by the Addisons out at Crossrigg Hall and the Slacks at Bewley Castle. There were several other yeoman farmers, but their acreages were mostly considerably less than 100 acres. So it is to be assumed that the Dents were relatively prosperous during the first half of the century.

The family had given money towards schooling in the village as early as 1782, and an earlier Henry had been churchwarden three times by 1800 and again in 1812. Soon afterwards, however, Henry allowed his home to be used by Methodist preachers, and in 1818 the family gave away part of their garden for the building of a chapel, together with £30 towards building costs.

The Methodist Chapel, Bolton and Elm House a century ago.

In 1833 a Sunday School was started, with Henry's son John Dent as its superintendent, and amongst those attending would surely be his own children, including the six year old Henry. This might account for some of the religious sentiments expressed in his later poetry and letters, and perhaps for the high level of literacy he attained. Unfortunately there seem to be no records of where the village school may have been situated before 1856, when a new building was erected on the village green, although a schoolmaster was amongst those listed in the Mannex directory of 1849. Often a curate would be responsible for teaching village children and it seems that in Bolton there may have been a school building not far from the Church.

Schooling in the first half of the nineteenth century was very haphazard, some villages having excellent schoolmasters who taught Latin as well as reading and simple arithmetic, and several Westmorland scholars found their way to Oxford and Cambridge Universities. There were private schools to which the more affluent might send their children and in Appleby there was already a Grammar School during this period, but there is no evidence that the Dent's sons attended there, though interestingly in the 1851 census Henry's younger brother John, aged 19, is listed as a student.

The village into which Henry was born was far more self sufficient than it is today, with occupations listed in the Mannex directory such as grocer, shopkeeper, butcher, joiner, miller, stonemason, blacksmith, tailor and shoemaker. There were also two inns and a beer house, though these would be anathema to the staunch temperance Methodists. The roads were rough and probably quite muddy in wet and winter weather. Most of the houses would have vegetable gardens or small garths with chicken runs or bee hives as well as flower gardens. Some former barns had been transformed into small cottages in what is now known as Silver Street, whilst near to the Dent's house, a short row of terraced houses had been erected in the early years of the century. A large new rectory was also built opposite the church with a commanding view over the Eden valley, and the bridge over the Eden was relatively new. At the centre of the village was the blacksmith's premises, where young and old would gather to watch the horses being shod, cart wheels formed or repaired and iron implements forged.

Farm work and the transport of people and goods was all by horse power, but even in this remote area all this was gradually to change with the coming of the railways. As early as 1836 a link from Preston through to Glasgow was envisaged, but in the depression of the 1840s it was hard to raise the enormous sums of money needed. Then a route had to be determined across the difficult terrain of Westmorland and Cumberland. At first it was proposed to tunnel under Orton Scar and take the line through Bampton and Askham, but this was dropped in favour of the Lune Gorge and Shap Fell route, despite the challenge of a 1 in 75 gradient. By January 1845 there were 4000 navvies and 400 horses at work not far from Bolton.

Henry and his youthful contemporaries must surely have been curious and excited about this innovative development, but sadly there are no poems on this theme in his book. By December 1846 there was a double track railway open all the way from London to Carlisle, two years later to Glasgow. The nearest station to Bolton was at Shap, only about 10 miles away. However, in 1847 Henry seems to have been more interested in the natural world than in railway engineering.

Henry the poet

The poetry notebook shows Henry to be a remarkably literate and thoughtful young man, given to solitary walks in the countryside. Although the first page of the notebook states that the poems were never intended for public perusal, Henry must have spent considerable time copying them out in his beautiful script. He started the book during the summer of 1847 and it may give some insight into his character and state of mind, although he protests that

"The following scribblings were done merely for amusement and shall never be put into any other form than that which they at present assume until they are reduced to their chymical element by fire: the writer of them never had, even in his wildest flights of imagination the slightest thought that he should ever excel in versification nor did he even think himself "somebody" who could successfully court the Muses; but he felt and then wrote to gratify his own inclination to amuse those around him; some may condemn his choice of subjects as being low, to those I would say, he had no choice but merely sang any theme that presented itself to his mind. If any should deem them worth a perusal they will doubtless condemn the sentiments of his letters to JC and say that time is too valuable to be squandered away in such a frivolous "word war" as is here fought. Truly time might be better employed than in concocting papers in the sentiment of which one can no more concur than think of being door keeper for the man in the moon, nevertheless as an amusement for a ladish mind it may be looked over, seeing that exercising the mind in this manner is much better than spending the few leisure hours of a practical agriculturalist at the Public House as many do."

Such versifying may not have been as unusual as it seems to us today. A local weekly paper, the *Cumberland Pacquet*, published two or three poems in each edition. The so called Lake poets, Wordsworth et al, were at work not far away during Henry's childhood, and at school many poems would have been memorized. Henry would also be very familiar with the hymns of John and Charles Wesley and others in the Methodist hymnal, and he obviously had access to books, as he mentions Milton, Pope and Byron. He had a lot of time to think whilst traversing the fields behind a plough or a harrow, and must have put pen to paper at evening in the privacy of his room. Maybe his position as the eldest son of the most prosperous farmer in the village also set him a little apart from others, as one of his poems laments the fact that three girls failed to acknowledge his greeting when he passed them in the street.

He was not without friends, however, as he begins his book with a sentimental poem "*To a friend; written on the evening of his wedding day*", and this is followed by "*The Lovers' Address*", where he dreams of a sweetheart "*surpassing all beauty*" and uses clichéd phrases such as "*zephyrs of the night*" and "*kind Cupid*". Then comes a jolly poem entitled "*The Old School Bell* " addressed to the inhabitants of Bolton, some verses of which run as follows:

In days of yore, when I was new
On almost every morn,
I sounded, and the breezes blew
Along the vales my tone.

The scholars at a distance I
Warn'd when the master came:
Some used to smile and others sigh,
Whene'er they heard my name.

.....
At noontide I was ever true,
To time as I could be;
As watches in those days were few
Amongst the peasantry.

So I their office did fulfil,
And told both saint and sinner,
That hedged, or ditch'd, or plow'd the hill,
When they might go to dinner

Many of the poems reflect religious sentiments, with references to toil and grief whilst on earth, and a belief in and longing for the everlasting bliss of heaven. The first poem addressed to Mr J.C. (his uncle John Crosby) is "*occasioned by the death of his son William, who was drowned in the river Eden, May 1848*".

Annoyingly, the poem's 26 stanzas make no mention of how the accident occurred and would be of little comfort to a bereaved father today.

Feeling Father of the hapless youth,
Be not o'ercome with too much sorrowing,
But from God's book of sacred truth,
Be still some ray of comfort borrowing.

Deplorable, 'tis true, this prank of Fate,
'Twould force the stoic into sighs:
What blighted hopes, - what prospects great
Now with him in oblivion lies.

He in oblivion? Nay, that cannot be:
There's a bright world succeedeth this,
He's merely from the body free,
Living (we trust) in endless bliss.

Not all the poems are in such a serious mood. The long '*Postscript*' to one entitled '*Lines suggested by the sight of a plant in a cottage window*' contains a lively narrative about a labourer who repairs to an inn after a hard day's work and calls for a "*glass o' gin*".

This being drunk off, an old tried friend
Comes in, his extra cash to spend;
To whom he owes a debt,
And takes a course of conversation
Which merely is an ostentation
For "Can you pay me yet?"

He then begins to scratch his ear,
And say "provision's very dear,
And somewhat scarce the chink:
Moreover Peggy's late been ill,
And Doctor's, faith, you know are still
Good hands at pen and ink."

"Why never lay't to heart good man,
I know you'll pay me when you can:
Waiter, bring here some hot ale."
They get a pint, to sweeten care
And after that, perchance they share,
A rousing brandy bottle.

Then thoughts of home the labourer haunts –
His anxious wife – his children's wants,
All flash upon his mind.
So off he sets, with hurry great
Caressing in his mind his mate,
That ever has been kind.

He reaches home, but strange to say,
His wife's dire passions 'gin to sway,
When merry airs he shows. –
She gives him such a reprimand,
As even courage could not stand
Without a dread of blows.

'Tis hard, nay passing hard to toil
As constant as the worm in soil
And ne'er forget our woes:
If this be reason in a wife
Pray have done with married life
And all the flowers it grows.

Indeed, old man, 'tis time to stop
If that be all you have to prop
Your present sad condition:
The man you talk of laboured hard,
And so does many a vile black guard
That well deserves derision.

Perhaps that day he half a crown
Had earned, and two and six gulped down
Before he reach'd his home.
Now where's his wife to get her bread,
And how're the children to be fed
E'en when there is no storm.

Surely there's a good excuse,
For women if they do abuse
Such men as this a bit.
'Tis strange, yet not more strange than true
You've opened out the very clue
I wanted you to hit.

If husbands wish to be beloved
Those magic feelings must be moved,
By showing kindness first
And not by irritation stern,
Or else the woe is sure to turn
Upon themselves the worst.

A large part of the poetry book, however, is given over to a correspondence in verse between Henry and his uncle John Crosby, which seems to have been stimulated by a remark by the latter that he was sorry that Henry was so lonely. The correspondence starts in June 1847 and continues throughout the Summer, the letters presumably carried between Bolton and Kirkby Thore by the new postal service, as some of the replies written bear the very next day's date. Henry undoubtedly copied these letters into his book at a later date, as the poem mentioned earlier concerning the death of John Crosby's son in 1848 is on an earlier page than some of the verse letters dated 1847.

I love o'er lofty wilds to stray,
At morning or at close of day.
It yields a thrilling joy!
Or on some lonely path to tread,
When the pale moon has heaved its head;
Much company's but annoy.

I love to stray by Eden's streams,
And ponder o'er my 'waken dreams;
'Tis pleasure to my heart!
There I could almost wish to spend
My leisure hours – serene, my friend
What else can joy impart?

The busy world with all its noise
Cannot impart such pleasing joys!
Vain counterfeit at best!
And they who mingle in its strife,
Know nothing of the joys of life;
They ne'er are truly bless'd.

Far better 'tis to walk alone
Than be of pleasure barely shorn,
By bustling crowds of men!
What company is there half so good,
When straying in a lonely wood,
As the poor harmless wren?

It sits and plays its warbling tongue
O'er its beloved harmonious song;
Or hops from tree to tree;
What pleasure more can raise its heart
Above the reach of dull care's smart
Than to behold such glee?

I also love to see the flower
That's spread by God's unerring power
Along the wide spread meads!
A beauty on its bosom glows,
What can't be equalled by the rose
Or men's best garden weeds.

I love such scenes as now I view;
When gently falls an evening dew,
Upon the thriving herb.
All nature seems so fine and gay,
I do not hesitate to say
To pleasure there's no curb.

If you've felt sorrow dear John,
That I should seem so much alone,
Let now your sorrows end!
And if your hint I've not guess'd right,
Give me't in rhyme some future night,
And I'll remain your friend.

H Dent
Bolton, Saturday night June 19th 1847.

The Answer

Henry dear I've read your rhyme,
And candid say it is sublime,
But I would have you know;
That the joys of which you speak,
In my opinion are but weak:
Yea, meagre and quite low,
Compared with that of which I'll tell
Though heightened by your rural dell
Or some sweet private walk.
What sort of company's a poor wren,
For active sociable young men?
I wonder at your talk!
Why, don't birds of like feather
Always meet and flock together,
If forsaken how they moan!
If other company you'll not seek
Your joys at best will be but weak,
And you'll remain alone.

When God made man and placed him; where?
In Eden's Garden, yes, e'en there,
Where pleasure flow'd unrent,
He found himself mateless, - alone,
To share his comforts there was none,
Nor could he be content. –
The Lord of love saw his sad case,
And by his side he soon did place,
The sweetener of his life
A beauteous, smiling mate to him was given,
The best and greatest boon of Heaven,
A lovely wife. –

So when you take your walks again,
And view the dell or feather'd train
You'll not forget it soon,
There's no companion for you there,
They'll teach you, you should also pair,
And not remain alone.

I love when by running streams I walk
To have a friend with whom I talk,
And tell them all my care;
One that's ready to share my fate,
And all my joys reciprocate,
And half my burden bear. –

Though I with you may love to roam
In woods and glens, around our home,
Or 'side Eden's streams, to take our rest
When the pale star looks on its breast,
Our spirits then will take the tone
And sigh that we are all alone: -
I've none to smile when I am free
And when I sigh to sigh with me. –

So Henry now you'll take this pill,
Send me a stronger if you will:
But I must know in rhyme before 'tis late
How this of mine doth operate.

To H Dent Bolton   J Crosby   June 20ᵗʰ1847

To this Henry replies that woman cannot be seen as *'Heaven's best boon'* as Eve tempted Adam and ate of the forbidden fruit which brought sin into the world. She is a *'vile deceiver'* and he doubts whether a virtuous woman can be found *'amongst the flowers on British ground, much less in Yankey land'.* John responds in defence of Eve, saying Adam was as much to blame, and pointing out that

'Twas women that made Christ a feast,
And welcom'd him as their best guest:
And these our saviour loved.-
'Twas women that stood by his side,
And wept when he was crucified,
While others faithless proved.

And continues

For what's a man without a wife?
He's like a tree that has no life,
Or half a pair of sizzars –
He's like a house without a door,
And a nut that has no core
Or ale that never fizzars.

So choose you out a handsome wife,
And one who is not given to strife,
And equal in age and purse –
One who's given God her heart and by her actions
You may see that you've her affections:
You must not do much worse.

Five days later Henry replies, excusing the delay by explaining that had he replied immediately he would have risked their friendship with an immoderate response. He now accuses John of quoting the words of someone called Kirke White.

Henry Kirke White is little known today, except for some hymns that are still in use, but he was someone with whom Henry may have felt a kinship, as he was of lowly origins, the son of a butcher in Nottingham, born in 1785 and died of tuberculosis in 1806. A very bright child, he attended school from the age of 3, and went on to the Nottingham Academy at the age of 7, where he was a contemporary of Byron. He wrote poetry from an early age, his 500 line poem entitled *Clifton Grove* appearing when he was 16. He was admired by Byron, Southey, Wordsworth and Browning. Some lines from *Clifton Grove* may offer an insight into Henry Dent's favoured style:

> *The pale mechanic leaves the labouring loom*
> *The air-pent hold, the pestilential room.*
> ...
>
> *Here lonely wandering o'er the sylvan bower,*
> *I come to pass the meditative hour.*

The subject of *Clifton Grove* is a faithless maiden who fails to wait for the return of her plighted lover, but weds another in his absence.

Henry responds with a long unattributed quotation, probably from Lord Byron, who has loved '*above a score*' of women, so Henry thinks Byron can best tell whether women can be true. The quotation ends with the line: "*Woman, thy vows are traced in sand*". Henry then rather boldly suggests to his preacher uncle that he should take out his Bible and read the history of how Samson was robbed of his strength, David was led astray and King Solomon was deceived by women. Surely, he argues "*Of all the boons with which we're bles'd, The gift of God's dear Son's the best.*"

The argument goes on into August, with John pointing out that God's son was not given until well after the time of Adam and

Eve, so that the dispute over Heaven's best boon is fruitless, but Henry will not let the matter rest, and the debate goes on. The arguments become more and more abstruse, with John eventually listing all seven of Henry's points one by one and pointing out their fallacies. He begs Henry to admit his errors and suggests that in a month's time they each produce a poem on the subject of 'Woman' and make that an end to the matter. Henry doesn't comply, however, and the verses ramble on. Rather like in a university tutorial, he seems to be arguing for the sake of it, knowing that his points don't really stack up.

At the end of the book are a few free standing poems penned by Henry, but undated. One is a rebuke to three young ladies who failed to respond to his greeting when he passed them by. He accuses them of the sin of pride. Another is addressed to '*B, M and H occasioned by their presenting me with a nose-gay, each one making a part*'. Perhaps these were the same three young ladies, stirred by the earlier rebuke? The flowers may die after a short time, but
'*Friendship and love are not yet dead/Nor shall they ever be*'.

'*The Christian's Farewell*' is another rather sentimental poem, reminiscent of a hymn, and '*On the Death of a Happy Child*' contains lines that are hard to understand in this more secular age. However, in the poem entitled '*Where is the Place and Who is He?*' Henry seems to reveal more of his true state of mind.

I feel in my breast
A disturbance of rest,
Ah what can the cause of it be?
I'll bear it in mind
And study to find,
The cause of this trouble in me.

Is it that I'm lonely,
And friends possess only,
When self-interest bears rule in the breast?
O no, I have some
Who if trouble should come
Would feel, and be deeply oppress'd.

Is it that I'm old,
And the grave soon must hold
This body of mine in its cell?
No, for to speak truth
I am blooming in youth
And in body I'm perfectly well.

Then whence are those sighs,
That so constantly rise,
And dash my sad heart with their spleen?
They derive their promotion
From a heart rending notion,
That my future abode I've not seen.

Could I but discern
My fate, I'd not mourn,
But joyfull and chearfull would be:
My heart would be light,
If once I'd had sight,
Of the place and the lover for me.

Then where is the place,
And whose is that face
Which now is o'erspread by time's wing?
Ah! Here I'm lost,
By commotion I'm toss'd
For the thought in my heart is a sting.

Begone the dull thought!
It availeth me nought:
No more will I dare to repine.
What if God doth take care
Of the birds of the air,
He surely will my lot assign.

If these are Henry's true feelings, there is something of a puzzle here. He asks *where is the lover*, but the title asks '*who is he?*' Does this imply that Henry craves the love of a man, and is this partly the reason for his long dispute with John Crosby over the attributes of women? Obviously this cannot now be ascertained, but it might explain why his book was kept in secret and '*doomed to the flames*', for Henry would have been deeply ashamed if this knowledge had reached his family. It might also have been the spur for him to leave his home village, despite being the eldest son and likely heir to a prosperous farming business.

Henry goes to London

Nothing more of Henry's life is known until 1851 when there is a letter from him to his father dated July 9th with the address given as 24 Warren St, Islington. It is apparent that John has paid for Henry to visit London and that he has stayed in the capital for two weeks, some of the time accompanied by his cousin Thomas Rigg from Milnthorpe. He also mentions that John Smith and Mr Dalton have been very kind in *"showing me anything they could."* The address in Islington is intriguing, as there is no longer a Warren St there, only the well known street near Euston Station. However a map of 1824 shows a short lane of that name to the west of the confluence of Liverpool Road and Upper Street, just north of the current Chapel Market, so it would seem that he may have been staying with friends who lived there.

The magnificent Euston Station with its Doric pillared portico was already the terminus of rail lines leading to the north of England and Henry would certainly have arrived there. He does not describe the sights and sounds of London in any detail in this letter, except to say that *"I should like to live in London after all if I had a business but I would not for the world spend my life as I have done this fortnight. Labour is a rest compared with running about sightseeing"*. Of course the only way he could get about the capital was on foot, or by horse drawn cab, but that cost more money, and he was trying to be as economical as possible, so he must have walked many miles. On this July day he walked to the station with Thomas Rigg *"thinking to see him off home, but the newspapers had misled us. There was no second class carriage attached to the train so rather than pay 56 shillings for the passage to Milnthorpe, he determined to stay till tonight."* Train timetables were printed in the newspapers in those days, but then as now, they were subject to last minute changes!

Henry then described his day:

"I took a tour down Regent St to Westminster Abbey. Regent St is certainly the grandest thoroughfare I ever saw, and indeed some far travelled men recon it the <u>finest street in the world.</u> On my way I visited the National Gallery and saw many fine drawings, passed the Duke of Wellington's monument in Trafalgar Square, the far famed White Hall and reached the ancient Abbey. This is splendid. There are monuments here that cost many thousands and the place keeps good time with its contents. After this I got into a jumbling mass of people all anxious to get into the House of Lords – it being open to the public today – at least professedly so. There was little pleasure there – we had to wait at the entrance a long time before admittance could be obtained at all, then after walking near a quarter of a mile through courts and aisles were stopped by door keepers here and there the crowds being so great. However at length I managed to reach the spot where our great men transact their business, and certainly such a gorgeous place it is that if you suffer your imagination to picture a fairy palace I dare be bound to say it will fall far short of the reality. I intended here to gather some knowledge but the crowds of people rendered it quite impossible. I could not even hear what the subject of debate was. After I left this scene I took the steamboat down to London Bridge and made my way to the Tower to pay Rob Langmire another visit."

It seems that this Rob Langmire had borrowed money from the Dents, but he was still not in a position to pay it back. Maybe he was a serving soldier billeted in the Tower. The previous evening Henry reports that he had attended a Wesleyan Reform meeting in Exeter Hall – *"It was an enthusiastic meeting but I did not stay to the end as I was <u>alone</u> and had a great distance to travel after coming out."* Presumably he did not want to be walking alone to Islington after nightfall for fear of being mugged.

Continuing the letter the next morning Henry says that Mr Smith called on him the previous evening and they went down to Cheapside to see a royal procession "*but the crowds were so immense there was no seeing any procession. The streets were set with soldiers about 11 yards apart I suppose from Buckingham Palace to Guild Hall. These were to prevent the way from being blocked up. Every street that led into the way was barred by a rail and in some place six or seven policemen to keep back the crowd. I heard that when the Queen passed there was the most enthusiastic greeting for her in every quarter. The streets were illuminated in a manner I never expect to see again. We got home about 1 o'clock this morning and were very much fatigued. I feel rather jaded this morning.*" Nevertheless he proposed to go down towards Bow Church "*to an institution where they keep all the periodicals (of any note) in the Kingdom, from there to take my final farewell of the grand exhibition and leaving that call at the Wesleyan Reform Bazar in Hanover Square, from thense to the Poletechnic Institution in Regent St, then I shall be ready for "Nature's sweet restorer", balmy sleep.*"

The exhibition Henry mentions here is of course the Great Exhibition of the Works of Industry of All Nations opened by Queen Victoria and Prince Albert on May 1st. Housed in Joseph Paxton's innovative Crystal Palace in Hyde Park, the exhibition attracted visitors from far and wide. At first the entry fee was such that only the wealthy upper classes could afford to attend, but at Prince Albert's insistence 'shilling days' were introduced from the end of May and there were even some special railway excursion rates of 5 shillings return from the north of England. History books all mention the Great Exhibition of 1851 as a watershed moment in the nineteenth century. The era of the Napoleonic wars was over, the economy had survived the downturn of the 1840s, the British Empire spanned the globe, and trade and industry were booming thanks to its entrepreneurial and inventive citizens. Was a visit to the Exhibition the prime purpose of Henry's visit to

London? Certainly it would account for the crowds of people he mentions more than once in this brief letter. Perhaps he had already described his visit to the Crystal Palace in a letter which has not survived. There was so much to see there that he made more than one visit, but it would have been interesting to know which exhibits he found most interesting; innovations in farming equipment perhaps, or more exotic items from far off lands. Amongst these was a single nugget of gold from South Australia, amongst an array of other minerals from that colony. The newly formed colony of Victoria only displayed a bag of flour, a contribution easily passed over.

There is a hint that Henry was at loggerheads with his father, as he says that perhaps the family is getting along *"better without (me) in one sense than you would with me but on the whole perchance I might be found of some service. This is an era in my existence I shall ever have to look back to with pleasure and thankfulness to you for favouring so unworthy a creature as me with the means of going through it."*

The letter finishes on a practical note, asking that one of his brothers may be allowed to come to meet him when he returns from London. He will arrive in the forenoon and walk towards a farm called Winter Tarn. *"Perhaps it would be best to start from Bolton after dinner and come by Sleagill, and if I feel able I will walk a little bit to meet them but I fear I shall be up by reaching the Tarn."*

Writing on Thursday morning, Henry says: *"Tomorrow after rambling about a little I yet know not when I shall start for Westmoreland."* Assuming he was not going to ramble about at night time, and he expects to be in the north before noon, he must be intending to take a night train, as the journey took at least nine hours, or slightly less for express trains, but those had no second class carriages. A Bradshaw guide dated 1849 shows a train leaving London at 8.45pm which reached Shap at 7.40am the next day. Intending to walk to Winter Tarn,

Henry would certainly be "*sufficiently stru*" to appreciate a lift from a cart brought by one of his brothers. Incidentally, the single second class journey in 1849 cost thirty three shillings and sixpence, a not inconsiderable amount added to Henry's expenses during this two week holiday.

What tales he would be able to tell his brothers and sister about London and his great adventures there.

Henry makes a decision

While London in 1851 was the scene of great rejoicing in the power and success of the British Empire, on the other side of the world developments were taking place which would have massive repercussions in many British households. The word on everyone's lips in Australia was gold, traces of which had been noted earlier, but in February 1851 indisputably so. The find at Bathurst, New South Wales, was officially announced in Sydney by the Colonial Governor the day after London's Great Exhibition opened in May, but this was not known in England until at least four months later. The first Australian gold rush was composed of farmers, shepherds, clerks and trades people from all over the Australian colonies, as well as freed convicts, particularly 'Vandemonians' from over the water in what would later be named Tasmania.

Coinciding with the planned separation (of July 1851) of the southern part of New South Wales to form the new colony of Victoria, an economic crisis loomed, due to the depopulating rush to Bathurst from an area which numbered only 77,000 people. The solution of the new administration in Victoria was to form a Gold Discovery Committee to encourage the search for gold on Victorian territory. Success came in late July when huge deposits were found at Ballarat. Soon between 6,000 and 10,000 diggers had converged on the area, and the Victorian gold rush was on.

News of all this filtered very slowly back to Britain, however, because mail took so long to arrive by sailing ship. However, in the first three weeks of April 1852 six ships arrived in London carrying between them eight tons of Victorian gold. Every newspaper in the land carried this sensational story, and suddenly everyone wanted to know "*where Australia is*". The era of Australia being seen merely as a repository for the dregs of British society had at last come to an end and the efforts already being made, through an assisted passage scheme, to send out farmers and tradesmen to populate the empty spaces on the map was superseded by voluntary emigration on an unprecedented scale.

The assisted passage scheme to the colonies, designed to take the labouring classes overseas to work for the growing British Empire, had been in operation for some years and migration commissioners travelled the length of the country trying to sign up able bodied men.   They also published a Colonization Circular each month, giving details of the conditions in each colony, the cost of passage from principal British ports, prices of many items in the different colonies and useful information as to what the emigrant might need to take with him.   In June 1852 the section headed Demand for Labour – New South Wales, states:

"*In a return dated 8th November 1851 the Immigration Agent at Sydney reports as follows:-*
In consequence of the recent discoveries of extensive gold fields in this colony a large proportion of the labouring population has been attracted thither, and therefore drawn away from their ordinary occupation. An increased demand consequently exists for all descriptions of labourers and mechanics. Of the former, those most in demand are shepherds, farm servants, agricultural labourers, and female domestic servants.   Of mechanics, those in demand are such as are engaged in the erection of buildings;   viz., masons, bricklayers, carpenters and blacksmiths."

Of Victoria, the report says simply: "*The demand for labour and the kind of labourers required appear to be much the same as in New South Wales.*"

These official reports were severely out of date before their publication, but nevertheless in the last week of May 1852 2,500 emigrants left Liverpool for Victoria in just three ships. The sensational newspaper reports from April 1852 onwards of gold being discovered in Victoria ensured that the greatest number of emigrants were attracted less by the prospect of working as farm servants and mechanics than by that of making a fortune from gold. Young men flocked to the ports from every county of England, including Westmoreland, where Henry Dent must have read the articles and felt that here at last was an opportunity to make a new life for himself. Another young man, living in the neighbouring village of Cliburn, came to the same decision. This was Henry Richardson, 22 year old son of a schoolmaster, who was listed as a 'scholar' on the electoral roll of 1851. Henry D. does not mention this companion in his earlier letters, though he writes of 'we' so it is to be assumed that the families knew that the two Henrys were travelling out together. In later letters 'Mr Richardson' is often mentioned, and it is this Henry who breaks the tragic news later. The passenger list for the ship on which Henry Dent sailed is held in the Victorian State archives and it confirms that Henry Richardson was indeed on board, along with 'Harry' Dent.

Another contributory factor may have been a letter received in Westmoreland from a Mr John Palmer, who was very likely a friend of John Dent. This letter is quoted in a book entitled 'The Gold Finder of Australia' by John Sherer, but unfortunately the beginning is missing, so it is not entirely certain when it was written or to whom. John Palmer was from the village of Glassonby, not too far from Bolton, and having married Ellen Shearman from Orton, he had a large family of sons. He emigrated at the end of the 1840s and acquired 200 acres of land soon after landing, the first Crown Land to be auctioned off in that area by the New South Wales Government. His letter stresses the great opportunity for a strong and industrious family to make a good living. The discovery of gold a few miles north of his homestead at Kyneton was an unexpected bonus which enabled him to build a substantial two storey stone house, which he called 'Glassonby'. (see postscript p 72)

Henry at sea

Henry was quick off the mark. By early July 1852 he was writing to his parents from the ship named the 'Serampore' as she lay at anchor in the 'River Mercy' awaiting permission to set sail for Australia. Perhaps he had seen an advertisement in the London Times of May 22nd 1852 which stated that the Serampore would sail for Sydney on June 26th. Or perhaps there were agents locally who advised him on how to book a passage. All the ship brokers in Liverpool and elsewhere were desperate to charter vessels to meet the sudden rush of passengers to Australia and to carry supplies there. The Serampore was chartered by Gibbs Bright and Co from W S Linsey of London and was a comparatively new ship, though still powered entirely by sail. Later, iron hulled ships, powered first by paddles and later by screw, would prove larger and faster. In the event the Serampore did not set sail until 6th July and the destination was Melbourne, not Sydney. Henry's brother John was at Liverpool to see the ship "glide through the locks in Princes Dock. I stretched out my hand and shook yours on the bounds of our native land."

In a letter begun on Sunday July 4th Henry reports that there were about 220 passengers and 45 crew, which was comparatively few, the standard number for most ships being 300-350 persons. The passengers having embarked on the ship, it was then "tugged up the river about one mile, where we cast anchor and waited for the inspection of the surgeon. He came in the afternoon and summoned us upon deck. When he called over our names and simply asked us if we were quite well I think we all answered in the affirmative." It was a requirement that a surgeon sail with each emigrant ship to ensure the health of the passengers. Where a ship carried emigrants under the assisted passage scheme, the ship owners would only be paid for passengers actually arriving at their destination, so there was an incentive to minimize loss of life through illness or injury during the voyage. Many surgeons' logs have been preserved to this day and provide a valuable insight into shipboard conditions.

Another delay was caused by having to wait for a government inspector to check the number of passengers, as a previous Gibbs Bright ship had been overloaded and the extra passengers were obliged to wait for the *Serampore* at the company's expense. Whilst these laudable checks were being made, the captain and several of the crew remained on shore, but Henry was complimentary about the mate, who was left in charge.

On the Tuesday morning a steam tug arrived and all the passengers were called up on deck for a further name check, which revealed that two first class and four second class passengers were missing. Henry thought that they had gone on shore, not expecting the ship to set sail until the next day. They would be left behind while their luggage went on before them! Henry gives further details in a later letter which his family would not read until many months later.

"We were taken in tug by a steamboat down the river Mersey about 3pm on Tuesday July 6th and about 12 all sail being set a gentle NNW wind took us smoothly along. Many amused themselves with shooting at the porpoises, seagulls and diving ducks which are seen in abundance in the Channel. Friday 9th at 6pm passed Cape Clear. (St George's Channel lies between the coasts of Wales and Ireland, Cape Clear is the most southerly point of Ireland) *This day I first experienced the sensation of sea-sickness which was attended by violent head ache. Instead of going down to dinner I went upon the forecastle, laid down and with my hands upon the jib chains,*

face over the rolling waves had a good vomit. I managed to take a cup of tea in the evening and retired at an early hour."

Writing before the voyage got under way, Henry had been full of praise for onboard arrangements:

"We are very comfortably situated and are just getting arranged into messes of a dozen each to sit down to table together. We have a messman at the head of each table who deals out an equal quantity of what is laid before us. We have about a dozen biscuits brought to the table of the size of a good bason top and half an inch thick. Cans of coffee are brought and the allowance of butter. He with a table knife places the butter upon the biscuit and the parties spread it themselves. Two cups of coffee is the allowance. We don't allow any to leave table till all have done and so we avoid confusion by another stepping in. By this system the messman and his party all leave table together. Yesterday we dined on salt beef, soup and half a biscuit each. On Saturday we had fresh beef to dinner and there was more than required. We breakfast at 8 in the morning, dine at 12.30 and tea about 6. "

This timetable and mess system was standard on emigrant ships. It seems that Henry travelled as an '*intermediate*' passenger, neither cabin class nor steerage, probably sharing a large dormitory in what he calls the "*young man's department*". He had not applied for a government assisted passage so he probably paid £20, (the price quoted in the Colonization Circular of 1852) which was to include provisions supplied by the shipping company. Henry had been supplied with a list of these supplies before sailing, but had also taken the precaution of taking some extra eatables with him.

As soon as the ship sailed, complaints began to surface about the rations. On October 2nd whilst at sea in the Indian Ocean, Henry wrote in detail to his family about shipboard conditions:

"*While we were in the river our attendance was pretty good but now we began to find that we were at sea and must rough it. Our victuals were hardly cooked and what rendered it less bearable, the knives, forks, plates and dishes were disgustingly dirty. The servants were inexperienced men, being working out their passage* (ie. steerage passengers)*, and even of those there were insufficient to wait upon the passengers. We agreed to have a meeting of the caterers of each mess. They drew up a petition to the Captain representing our case. He kindly received our deputation, but he said that he was sorry to say it was not in his power to do all that our case seemed to require. He would see that our victuals were better cooked but as for attendants he had no authority to appoint any.* (If the passengers wanted to appoint more, they could do so and pay them out of their own pockets.) *Mr Tulloch, the chief mate kindly engaged to give the cook a receipt* (recipe) *for our pudding and see that he got it and other things better cooked.*"

"*The dietary scale was pretty well adhered to in one sense but no better than it should be after all, for the quality of the beef was by no means good. In fact I and scores of others have never eaten an ounce of it since we sailed along St George's Channel. The pork is far from the standard of the ingredient that goes by that name in Westmorland. It has been preserved in pickle since – but I can't specify the time. However, I think I may safely say it was not done yesterday but some winter within the last ten years the Yankeys had found a little time to kill a few of their acorn fed hogs and barrel them up. This kind of thing I could very well dispense with during the hot weather but a little of it cold eats very well to a dry biscuit. However, Westmorland ham is better, and of this I have sufficient for the voyage and for a few days in Australia if the diggings should have produced a famine. The "fresh or preserved potatoes" mentioned in the bill of fare have turned out to be nothing but preserved potatoes. The peas are made into soup. The rice is boiled and with molasses eatable but far from the thing we used to call rice at Gill-flosh (i.e his home). The preserved beef is in tins – or rather was, for it is some weeks since we've had any. This was very good. The thing we now get in its place 3 times a week is what is called soup and bouilli. It is constituted of small pieces of preserved beef, turnips, onions and other vegetables and would have been good had we been upon our voyage about 1848, but it now tastes rather old and would not have been palatable had not many passengers brought eggs preserved in salt. (The shipping company had not provided salt for the 2nd class passengers) The tea on board is of tolerable quality, butter and sugar good. Coffee frequently spoiled by over roasting. The oatmeal is very coarse and has a peculiar taste which it takes a quarter of an hour's boiling to take off. This we boil ourselves and although porridge was looked upon as a sort of pig fare when we came on board by the majority of passengers, before we had been at sea a month it was looked to as a great relish and taken with a thankful heart by all who could succeed in getting it cooked. You will recall that the bill of fare stated that when fresh meat was served out there would be no issue of flour, rice, raisins, peas, suit or vinegar but 1lb of meat would be allowed to each adult. We had a meal of fresh beef while laying in the River Mersey. When we get the next it will be quite at our own option whether we have the other things to eat or not, for we shall have the market of Melbourne before us. "*

Henry does not mention the problem of drinking water, which was often very foul, leading to many emigrants drinking mainly beer or spirits if they could afford them, which led to inevitable consequences, even on a Sunday. Henry was incensed by the demeanour of some of his fellow passengers.

"I among the rest took my stand upon the quarterdeck while the Captain read the appointed prayers to which the passengers responded with all that gravity and sanctimoniousness so familiar to the iniciated hypocrite. How those who on

weekdays seem in their element while listening to and uttering "hell's horrid language" can on the Sunday assume such a devotional aspect is to me a mistery."

There was also drunkenness and fighting, even on a Sunday and Henry describes one such incident, which happened on Sunday August 6th when the temperature was 110F.

"In the afternoon a quarrel broke out between the Cook and one of the sailors. The storm had been brewing for some time and now the Cook had got too much spirituous liquor and was very much enraged. Williams, the sailor, was lying in a hammock near the galley. The Cook challenged him to a fight – he refused. The Cook kicked him out and he fell upon the deck and hurt his head which raised his passions to fighting point. They made a brutal afternoon, clashing each other against the bulwarks, tearing each other's hair and skin. Blood flowed freely. They could scarcely be separated either by the command of the Captain or the physical force of the passengers and crew. When separated the Cook intreated the Captain to let him have another round at Williams but was refused. Many remarks were made concerning the fight, none of which surprised me so much as those of the chaplain who said "It was a pity such a thing should occur on a <u>Sunday. He liked to see a good fight on a weekday as well as anyone but that was only bull dog work. However he should have liked to see them have another round</u>. (Henry's underling) That was rich was it not in one of the officers under the <u>Prince of Peace.</u> Since then I have never attended the prayers excepting once I was reading upon the bulwarks near the Poop and I reverently shut the book during the service." Henry's reading matter consisted of Dr Chalmer's sermons on cruelty to animals and on disseminating the gospel.

On a lighter note Henry tells of a newspaper that was started on board called the *Serampore* Gazette. It was hand written and there was only one copy, which had to be passed round under the proviso *"keep it clean and don't damage."* Henry wrote one article for it but was irritated to find it was broken off in the middle, and was to be completed in the following number. Maybe the editor was dismayed at Henry's verbosity or more likely the subject matter was none too popular, as his article was entitled *"The Canary – its struggle for liberty"*. Henry had been much cheered by the sweet singing of a ship board canary, which reminded him of the *"songsters of the groves in Old England which every breath of wind and every heavy wave wafted me from, perchance never again to witness."* However, one morning it escaped from its cage and could not be persuaded back in again. One of the passengers tried to throw his cap over it, but it flew off and *"alighted upon the waves for a rest, but they, unfaithful to all strangers, engulfed it in their foam and the poor canary was no more. As we passed its dead body we could not but revere the remains of one that nobly died in its struggle for liberty."*

By July 21st the ship entered the area of the North East Trade winds and flying fish were often to be seen in great flocks. *"On the morning of the 24th one was found exhausted in some chairs by the side of the vessel."* It was pinned up on a board for everyone to examine. *"It measured about 11" in length and its wing from tip to tip 12", in shape like a trout, its back blue, which on the sides gradually changed for white which was perfected on its belly".*

Henry did not find the weather as hot in the Tropics as he had expected, but conceded that the brisk winds helped to mitigate the heat on board. This would certainly be so up on deck, but surely the cabins below must have been stiflingly hot, and those in steerage quite foul with the odours of people crammed together in bunks with little sanitation. As the ship neared the Equator, the Trade winds ceased and *"we had to depend upon occasional breezes and varied winds."*

"Thursday August 12th – passed the "line". According to custom the sailors had what they call a jolly lark. Two of them were dressed up in grotesque attire and placed upon the Cannon's frame to represent Neptune and his wife. The others drew them in this chariot from the forecastle to the poop singing the song entitled "Rule Britannia". When they arrived at the poop they dismounted, presented the Captain with 2 fish, and received 5 shillings in return. They then collected from the passengers, receiving from two and sixpence to sixpence each. After this they drew water out of the sea and threw it upon all they came near, representing Neptune showering his blessings on us. In this the passengers heartily joined."

Sometimes other ships were sighted, occasionally sailing north, but none were near enough to pass on mail, and Henry's long letter was not posted until he reached Melbourne. Near the Cape of Good Hope there were beautiful sea birds and Cape pigeons, and later an albatross with a wingspan of 10ft was caught on a line baited with pork. The heat of the Tropics was replaced by freezing conditions as the ship headed south towards the Crozet Islands, only the second time they had seen land on the entire voyage. *"The latter we passed on the 17th of September. These presented a rugged appearance and were covered with snow. Since passing these we have had both frost and snow ourselves. Sometimes the vessel was covered as with a white mantle and upon the ocean looked like a solitary ghost. Some said we were in search of Sir John Franklin and even went so far as to ask the Captain if he did not think we were going too far south."*

This prompts Henry to suggest the kinds of clothing others might find useful:
"Let them provide clothing for both hot and cold weather. A good thick woollen rug would be useful for both kinds of weather. When hot they might take it upon deck to sit upon, and in the cold weather it would be useful as a bed cover. Parties ought to provide themselves with something very

warm for their feet as they cannot run to a fire when the snow falls and they scarcely can have exercise sufficient to keep warm. Let them have a pare or two of woollen socks to put either above or under their stockings and a pair of cork soals to keep their feet dry. These would be all the better if covered with flannel. I think the feet the most important as they will be sure to chilblain if not provided for. For my own part I did not anticipate such cold weather and had no cork soals so made a pair out of cotton wool and flannel which was vastly better than nothing yet notwithstanding this I felt my toes a little bitten though they never were before to my knowledge."

He also gives more advice on useful food provisions to bring along, such as cheese, ham and flour, as well as soda and tartaric acid which seem to have been used for purifying the foul drinking water. Quite a few items of food could be purchased on board as extras to the 'dietary scale' provided, and Henry details the prices to show how expensive they all are, and some provisions were long since exhausted. He cannily suggests that anything extra that people bring on board can also be sold to fellow passengers.

All in all, Henry's voyage was pretty tolerable, though he admits that there were several squalls and a gale in which some damage to the ship was sustained. Henry reports that there were no deaths, no contagious diseases and very little illness, a happy and unusual state of affairs on such a long and arduous journey.

When the Serampore finally reached the entrance to Port Phillip Bay on a Saturday evening in late September, she then had to wait until the Monday for a pilot to lead her over dangerous sandbanks, past several wrecks and up the 40 or so miles to Williamstown. This took about 6 hours. Already anchored at Williamstown "we found at least 200 vessels, most of which could not get men to take them to sea. Captains were offering £30 a month or £60 a run to China but not a man could they get." Captain Smith tried to pre-empt the loss of his sailors by raising their wages from £3 to £8 a month, but lost some anyway. The lure of the gold was just too great.

The passengers of the *Serampore* were rather lucky in that they insisted to the Captain that their tickets entitled them to passage into Melbourne itself, and he honoured this agreement, though Henry thought that he paid for their transport himself, the company agents being unwilling to pay. Many passengers found themselves on board ships which cast anchor at small settlements around the bay, from where they were at the mercy of unscrupulous persons who charged exorbitant amounts to transport them and their baggage into the town itself. After so many weeks at sea the sight, smell and feel of land must have been overwhelming.

Henry arrives in Australia

Henry's arrival in Melbourne was not auspicious. *"A thorough wet day it was -. the channels on each side of the streets flowing like rivulets."* However, Henry and his companion were lucky enough to have a contact, Mr Benn, who recommended them to lodgings at Mr Rhodes' in Lonsdale Street. Although the cost of 10 shillings a day each seemed rather high, they decided to stay there. This was probably a good move, as Melbourne was literally bursting at the seams.

In 1851, before the discovery of gold, Melbourne had a population of 23,000. By September 1852, the staggering number of 15,000 persons were arriving *every month.* Admittedly, many of these would only be passing through, but it is not surprising that many owners of property made as much money through renting out rooms and bed spaces as did some of the gold diggers from their physical labour. Sellers of provisions and equipment were also in a good position to make money quickly. The new state administration had hoped to build a beautiful city without cheap wooden weather boarded buildings which had a tendency to burn down. They planned a city of wide streets and handsome stone buildings, but the pressure for housing in 1852 meant a quick relaxation of this rule and wooden shanties were hastily thrown up. There was even a 'canvas town' south of the River Yarra which at one time housed 7000 homeless immigrants. Henry was therefore quite lucky to be able to afford decent lodgings in a central street for 10 shillings a day. Some landlords even charged for a bed space under or on a table in a room shared with many others.

Most would-be diggers did not intend to stay long in town. Indeed Mr Benn advised Henry and his friend to go straight to the diggings, even though the roads were still in a bad state at the end of winter. He would store their boxes, so that they could travel light, as the cost of hiring any sort of cart would be very expensive. The price of many items had rocketed with the unexpected demand. *"I was taking some things out of my chest to take up the country. A man came up and asked me if I had got any boots that would serve him to go up to the diggings in. I said that I had not got any for sale but I had two pairs of quarter boots and at present only wanted one. Well, what would I take? Would he like to have them for 25s. The money was laid down and he said that if they had been waterproof and two inches higher he would have had them at 35s."*

But first Henry wanted to visit a Methodist missionary at Collingwood, on the outskirts of Melbourne. This Mr Townsend had come out a few years previously and had purchased a very nice house, which appreciated substantially in value since the gold rush. He was also planning a new chapel to be built by means of subscriptions from successful diggers. At the other end of the scale Henry resolved to *"pry into the state of society"* in Melbourne, despite advice to keep indoors after 6pm *"and never to utter the word convict, at least disparagingly. In speaking of them we must use the term "Government men". We walked the streets for three hours after dark and met with the greatest civilities from all parties with whom we conversed. In fact I could see and have seen more wickedness in the streets of London in one hour than during the whole night here."* This was not to deny that there were crimes committed, but Henry put most of them down to the effects of the demon drink.

In conclusion of this first letter from Australia, Henry is optimistic that he has got to the right place, and thanks his father for *"his permission and means to come here"* but regrets that he did not come three or four years previously, as there is a good living to be made at many trades. *"A family of agriculturalists coming and settling near to some highway or river as they could reasonably purchase land by cultivating it, themselves might soon realize a fortune."* They would be able to sell their produce at very good prices due to the great and rising demand, as

"The numbers flocking here are out of all the bounds of my preconceived notions. About 20,000 arrive each week."

To the diggings!

Henry and his friend Mr Richardson probably set off for the diggings sometime in October, though the next letter home is dated December 1852. Their destination was not Ballarat, but the area of Mount Alexander, some 80 miles to the northwest of Melbourne. They had a useful contact to help them on their way, Mr Palmer, who had apparently received many favours from Henry's father and was most welcoming and helpful. His farm near the township of Kyneton, fifty miles from Melbourne, was doing very well with sheep and dairy farming, oats and wheat. His sons took turns to try their luck at the diggings, returning home to help at sheep shearing and harvest time. 'Glassonby' was a useful staging post between Mt Alexander and Melbourne, and the Palmer's hospitality proved very important later when Mr Richardson was suffering from dysentery.

The journey from Melbourne to Mt Alexander may seem comparatively short today, but it must be remembered that there was no surfaced road and the passage of bullock carts, horses and human feet led to extremely difficult travelling conditions, particularly after the winter rains. As Henry and his friend left many of their belongings behind with Mr Benn in Melbourne, they would be carrying only a few possessions on their backs and struggling along on foot, trying to avoid the worst of the mud. The sight of heavily loaded drays drawn by teams of eight to ten bullocks would be quite new to them, and they were probably shocked by the foul language of the drivers as they tried to persuade these recalcitrant animals to pull the heavy loads through the deep quagmires. Some of these drays were taking essential supplies to the diggings, such as flour, of which nearly half a million pounds were consumed per week.

On foot the journey took between seven and ten days, so it was necessary to camp overnight several times, the first stop usually being near to the settlement of Keilor, some twenty miles from Melbourne. Those with horses had to find feed for them and make sure they didn't wander off in the night, but Henry and his friend had only to make a camp fire to cook some food and put up a makeshift shelter of some sort, possibly under a tree, or using some leafy branches. A second day's journey of about 12 miles would take the traveller as far as Gisborne, where he could purchase a meal at the Bush Inn for 30 shillings or half an ounce of gold. (The landlord easily made a fortune from the passing trade.) It was considered sensible to overnight there rather than press on, because the next stretch passed through the notorious Black Forest, where dense stands of timber charred by bush fires in February 1851 made progress even more difficult and banditry was considered to be prevalent. Eight miles beyond the Black Forest lay the town of Kyneton, where the Coliban Inn was situated. Mr Palmer may well have supplied this busy inn with milk and meat from his farm, capitalizing in another way from the never ending stream of would-be diggers.

Whilst staying with Mr Palmer, Henry had a chance to consider the rumours already gleaned from other travellers about where best to set up camp once they arrived at the 'diggings'. 'Mount Alexander' referred to quite a large area, with several locations where gold had already been found. Maybe Mr Palmer's sons, who had already been at the diggings, could offer advice on where to go, or perhaps they accompanied the newcomers on this their first journey. Whatever the case, the friends travelled to the location of Fryer's Creek and pitched their tent at a place they called "Cumberland Row, Fryers Creek". The 'street' name is something of a joke as the area was certainly not laid out in any way like a town. Incomers pitched their tents wherever they could find a space, so Henry is probably alluding to the fact that several parties from Cumberland had chosen to stick together.

Lithograph of Fryer's Creek by S. T. Gill, 1852, courtesy of
National Picture Library of Australia

In the December letter, Henry describes their neighbours:
*"We are in good society, comparatively speaking and
surrounded by kind neighbours. Our nearest neighbour is a
gentleman from Northumberland of the name of Archibald who
left England in 1841 and has now a sheep station at Wimmera
200 miles up the country. His sons are now up shearing the
sheep. They are first rate neighbours and I sometimes go and
hold a yarn with him. Another neighbouring tent is inhabited
by a family of respectable persons named Adcock. They left
Cumberland about 2 years ago and have been keeping a
grocer's shop in Melbourne till last Summer. They came up
to the diggings and have done pretty well. Another family of
Watsons reside in our row who left Cumberland a month or
two before I left home. The bridge surveyor for the County of
Cumberland who perhaps you will know as a Wesleyan Local*

Preacher is this old gentleman's brother. Then there is Mr Palmer's tent containing Robert, John and William together with two of the Shearmans of Orton. (Mrs Palmer's maiden name was Shearman, so they were probably her brothers.) *The old gentleman Joseph Shearman (probably Mrs Palmer's* father) *was taken by the dysentery and was obliged to be taken down to Kyneton last week. We heard yesterday that he is no better and his two sons are off to see him. Two or three of the Palmers generally stay at the diggings about three months each end of the year."*

The hospitality offered by Mr Palmer was apparently so generous that
"Some indeed he has killed with kindness or in other words he has given them the requirements of Nature and entertainments of his house, refusing to receive remunerations till they sometimes passed his house without calling, when they would have been glad to have lodgings with him, if he would make a charge for it or receive a voluntary gift, but knowing that he has many visitors and that if they called he would receive no pay, they have chosen to travel on a little further. The old man seems to be disposed to do a good turn to any of his old countrymen or acquaintances and he is now in circumstances that he can well afford it. When we came up, the carriage of luggage was extremely high. Mr Palmer being gone to town I wrote him a note requesting him to bring up a chest containing some clothes of Mr Richardson's and my own. In case he should be too hard loaden I requested him to get it to some drayman in whom he had confidence and I would pay him on his return. On being down since his return I offered to pay the carriage. "Not one farthing" said he. "If I charged you anything for a job like that I would never forgive myself while I live. My family received many favours from your father in past times and I think of such things." He then told me that until I got settled I was to make his house my home and I should always be welcome. If at the diggings or anywhere else in the colony I should lose my health I was to make the best of time

43

in getting to his house and they would do all for me that laid in their power."

No doubt this assurance as to his physical welfare would be of great comfort to Henry's mother at home in Bolton, but Henry is also at pains to reassure his father on the question of his spiritual health. He seeks to justify his decision to seek gold, as many religious people were of the view that this was an *"unpardonable sin"*. He thinks such people would lose their prejudices if only they could visit the diggings, where they would find *"men of all classes of society and of nearly all trades and professions from the weaver who has left his loom to the lawyer who has quitted his wig. They'll find men of reputable character and sterling principle who have taken up the digger's pick and shovel and are anxious to make their fortune and "gather geese"*
"Not for to hide it under a hedge
Or for a State attendant
But for the glorious privilege
Of being independent."
And some I have no doubt from even higher motives than this, that they may be useful to their day and generation in dispelling darkness, ignorance and crime from the face of society both in their adopted country and the more privileged but still poor man's face-grinding England. It is true that there are bad characters on the diggings but not in so great a proportion as some are led to suppose. What part of the colonies would these individuals go to in order totally to escape bad company? May I not ask what part of England they could go to where every face they saw was unknown to them and still be confident they were in good company. In no place could they be sure of it. How much less then can they expect always to be in good company in a colony surrounded by penal settlements – a place not only having to contend with its own natural proportion of crime but with a hoard of profligates exported from England under the abominable system of conviction. These men are all that are to be feared upon the diggings and

at present I believe less crime is committed upon the diggings than in Melbourne and on the road".

In this first letter from Fryer's Creek Henry does not give much detail of life at the diggings, except to say that he and Mr Richardson have their own tent and *"cook and wash for ourselves"*. This tent may have been little more than a piece of canvas draped over a rudimentary frame made of poles cut from trees nearby. Larger parties, or those like the Palmers who had come from farms nearby, may have had more permanent structures. Cooking was done on an open fire of wood salvaged from any remaining copses of trees nearby, in an iron pot suspended over the flames from a tripod. A staple food for the diggers was a kind of unleavened bread called 'damper' which they cooked in the embers of the fire. Mutton was the most available type of meat, as sheep were driven to the camps and slaughtered at butcheries on the spot. Henry says that mutton was five and sixpence a hind quarter and four and six per forequarter that December, or a bit less *"if the sheep are thinner than usual"*. Potatoes, tea, sugar, bacon, cheese and butter were all available, but of course the price fluctuated according to the supply and demand, and the state of the roads. How much one could afford to buy depended on what funds the digger had at his disposal and his success in finding gold. Tools were also highly priced *"so you will easily conceive that it is useless parties coming here without a little money to begin with. It altogether depends upon the parties' fortune how much he should have for his upset. Some have to work long before finding anything, others drop on the gold at once. A labouring man coming up to the diggings ought at least to have £20 if he intends to make anything like a comfortable beginning."*

Henry was perhaps luckier than most in having such a useful friend as Mr Richardson, a companion with whom to share tent and tools as well as the hard work of digging. They had some early success in finding gold. *"We wrought 9 days and only* got 6dwts (penny weights). *Then we dropped upon a good hole and in about a week took 14 and a half ozs (ounces) out of it. After that we were a week before getting 1dwt. Last Saturday we marked out a place, sunk about 2 feet and on Monday put it down another 10 feet and have been mining it during the week. I think we have taken about 1lb (pound) out of it but we have not yet weighed it as we expect it will yield a few ounces more."*

In a postscript to the letter dated 5 days later he adds:
"Since I commenced we have been working the same hole and it yields us perhaps an ounce and a half of gold per day between us and so long as it will yield an ounce a day we will continue to work it, but if it falls under we will look out for another place."

For those unlucky in finding gold or unsuited to that type of work, Henry argues that farming would prove very lucrative, especially for a family with a little capital with which to buy land. They would have to bring their own implements, however, as most could not be obtained locally for love nor money. The enterprising immigrant should bring ploughs, carts and ironwork, as well as winnowing machines, churns, lead bowls, household and dairy utensils, and if he thought of settling near a town, milk kegs to fix to a horse's back. Mrs Palmer took milk down to Kyneton in this way and earned good money.

A second shorter letter to his father, also dated in December 1852, specifically asks if he can forward some farming equipment to Mr Palmer, which cannot be obtained locally.
"One single iron plough of the pattern Joseph Simpson has lately been making. It must have a pike sock and two extra mould boards.
One double iron plough to run on a plate in the centre and have mould board to widen or straighten according to the work required to be done.

Joseph Simpson's smithy in Bolton

One English winnowing machine.

These must be taken to pieces and those parts which can must be packed in a rough wooden case. The machine you might order to be made all ready and packed for exportation.

He likewise wants a peck of the best black oats and a few second early potatoes to raise a crop from. These things cannot be had here and he thinks they will answer first rate here. You will likewise much oblige by sending him as many hedgerow pippins as you can conveniently procure. These are to raise hedges from.

He likewise wants a dozen quartern corn scythes not of the patent manufacture and half a dozen round mouthed hedging spades.

If any one be coming whom you know about, you will do well to send them under these instructions "Directed to Mr Palmer, Care of Mr John Benn, Great College Street, West Melbourne".

He ends by saying that the cost of the goods and their freight should be invoiced to Mr Palmer and Henry will collect the money. If this is all too much trouble to his father, he suggests that brother John could do it, but in any event Mr Palmer has been so kind that he could not refuse such a request for help. Whether the order was ever fulfilled remains unknown.

'A tolerable idea of what the diggers really are.'

Henry said that this was his intention in writing to his brother John (who was now aged 21) in late December 1852 with more details of gold digging. First of all one had to purchase from the Commissioner a licence *"to dig, search for and remove gold from the Crown Lands of Victoria"*. This cost 30 shillings a month but without it, one could be fined a considerable amount. It entitled the holder to a plot measuring just 8ft x 8ft in which he might dig down anything up to about 50 or 60 feet in the search for gold. Labour such as this required considerable physical strength, and some men soon gave up. If they had heard tales of the early days when gold dust could be found in the roots of the grass or when nuggets could be found lying in the beds of the streams, this hard labour would have been even harder to bear.

"Many who are well qualified to handle a pick and shovel have been allured from their writing desk or counter at home by the hope of soon picking up on the diggings what will make them independent of work for the whole of their after life. Some of these are discouraged at first sight of the diggings and dare not face the labour requisite to obtain the gold. Others begin to dig and I have sometimes been amused to see them making their first efforts. They use the pick something like a young bird it's wings – very feebly. Some of these after sinking a few blank holes throw down the pick in despair and betake themselves to work for which they are more adapted. Others return to England, very likely with a bad report of the country when in fact the country is not to blame, but they are not adapted to its wants. "

Henry had no knowledge of geology or how gold was formed and in this he was no different from most other diggers. Indeed the first Australian gold was found entirely by chance, mostly on or near the surface. However, when the new State of Victoria officially sanctioned the search for gold, it was the experience of gold digging in the Californian gold rush of 1849 which stood many in good stead. The 'forty niners' could recognise certain features of the landscape, and through patiently sampling gravel in various creeks and streams they determined the most promising locations. Henry describes the Mount Alexander area as follows:

"On reaching the gold regions one of the first features that takes our attention is that of vast ridges of rock running North and South. These ridges stand on edge and often project out of the earth to a considerable height, but in general they are almost level with the surface. These rocks are of different kinds, some ironstone, some sandstone, and others slate rock. Another conspicuous feature in these gold regions is quartz covered hills. In some places these are quartz rocks, but for the most part it is lying in loose detached pieces upon the ground and forming rather an interesting sight especially as some of these pieces appear to have undergone a process of burning which has melted something out of them – either the gold itself or something essential to its formation. Gold is found in a variety of positions. Some mixed up with the surface soil, some in the beds of creeks, some scattered over large flats, generally covered in the first instance with gravel, and afterwards with black alluvial deposit. But at present about here the most gold is turning out of gullies. The sinking in these varies in depth from 15 to 40 feet and is mostly a very dry hard and speckled red and white clay mixed with soil and has evidently been washed down from the hills. Last summer large quantities of gold were taken out of hills some of which I have examined and found to vary vastly in the character of the earth and stone through which the holes are sunk. In one place where it has been very rich, in so much that it is nearly

all laid hollow and now standing upon wooden pillars and small walls and pillars of the original earth, it is a stange mixture of confused soil, red and white clay, a white semented rock of rather a freestone tendency and at the bottom, quartz stones and dross all semented up together so that a steel pointed pick will scarcely pearce it. Under this I am told there laid large quantities of gold and the diggers who got such places on working out their holes hastened down to town and acted upon the maxim 'lightly come, lightly go.' Many with whom I've conversed say they thought it would last for ever, but now it is not so easily found they have learned a lesson and would act differently."

The precise method of obtaining the gold is then described:

"On sinking a hole and coming to what the diggers think will contain gold they take a little into a tin dish and go to some water to try it. The first point is to bring it into a puddly state and then gently washing off the top, now and again shaking the dish so that if it contains gold it may sink to the bottom. If they come back with the report "no good" their men proceed to sink their hole still lower. On the other hand if they come across "stuff supposed to be gold" it is put into a large tub and water poured upon it. It is stirred about with a spade till it becomes a puddle, and the water is then poured off and renewed 3 or 4 times. After that the remaining dirt and stones is put in a cradle with a sieve underneath and water is gently poured on it while a person rocks the cradle with one hand and with the other hand stirs about the stones and dirt until the stuff is washed quite clean. Then they proceed to take out a slide board which has been placed under the sieve of the cradle in a slanting position, with a ledge on the bottom sufficiently high to catch the gold as it slides down the board and so low as to let most of the stones and lighter substances over, which by the rocking of the cradle and the force of the water are taken out at the bottom end of the cradle."

Dozens of holes might be sunk without finding any of the precious metal, but so long as others nearby were being successful, Henry remained optimistic. In March 1853 he reported that in the three months since he had started, only four of his holes had yielded anything, but one had produced 7lb 1oz in only six days. He was aware of some of the very large nuggets found at Ballarat that summer, one weighing in at the staggering 134lb 8oz. This was later exhibited in London. However, many men at Ballarat had found nothing at all! It took a special temperament to remain optimistic, and many men regularly drowned their sorrows in alcohol, the sale of which was actually illegal in the camps, though "*they allow any quantity under two gallons to be kept in each tent for private use. Notwithstanding this arrangement there are numerous sly grog shops.*"

At Christmas Henry had heard a disturbance outside his tent, shouting and swearing and the cry of "*My God, he's dead, he's dead*" but he did not go to investigate till morning, when he found a large patch of congealed blood upon the ground "*just as if a sheep had been sticked.*" . His policy was obviously not to intervene, as "*There are a lot of these Vandemonians,* (ie. from Van Diemans' Land – Tasmania*) the off-scouring of the British nation, who when their passions are raised by intoxicating drinks care not what they do. But this is far from the character of the diggers in general. They are upon the whole honest, industrious and well meaning men.*"

The keeping of the Sabbath was enforced by the authorities. This meant that no digging was allowed on Sunday. However, Henry also disapproved of those men who spent their Sundays shooting game, fetching firewood or spying out new digging areas. At first he and Mr Richardson walked the six miles to Forest Creek where there was already a Methodist mission, and later preachers came to Fryers Creek. Letter writing also took place on a Sunday, Henry asking his father to send him a small writing desk as he was using his copy of Shakespeare to rest upon. An incongruous picture springs to mind of this earnest young man in the digger's attire of striped shirt and moleskin trousers seated on a log outside his tent, pen in hand carefully composing his letters while resting his paper on the Bard's complete works.

On the whole Henry's four letters from Victoria paint a very civilized picture of gold prospecting which is very far from that given in other accounts. Conditions under canvas in the heat of the Australian summer were not ideal. There were dust storms and a serious problem when the water in the creeks fell very low, as it was used not only for panning the gold as described above, but also for drinking, laundry and all other purposes. Sanitation being non existent, it is hardly surprising that dysentery was very prevalent. The many butcheries where animals were slaughtered in the open air created a stench of rotting offal and plagues of flies. Meanwhile the entire landscape was devastated by the hundreds of holes dug and the spoil heaps around their edges, and deforested by the need for firewood and timber for tent poles. Soon after Henry Richardson succumbed to dysentery and went down to Kyneton, Henry decided to leave the diggings before winter rains made conditions even less tolerable.

Time to move on

The decision to leave the diggings was made partly because of Henry Richardson's illness and partly to try other ventures. In many of the letters, Henry urges others to come out to Australia, as there are many good opportunities in farming related activities. Farming at home *"is complete drudgery and life of toil for nothing compared with farming in Port Phillip. At home many an industrious and frugal farmer is embarrassed in his circumstances. Here all such are on the highway to independency and if things continue as they are they will not be long from being at par."* But he adds that prospective farm workers should bring their own equipment, ploughs, carts, winnowing machines, churns, lead bowls, household and dairy utensils to name but a few items.

However, acquiring land on which to farm was no easy matter in the new colony of Victoria, despite thousands of acres apparently lying empty. Most of the 60 million acres were in the hands of about 1000 so-called 'squatters' who paid the Government £20 per year for a long lease. Within a short time, many successful diggers who cherished an aspiration to secure an independent future, wished to purchase land, but the Victoria Government refused to bow to pressure to release squatters' lands to the highest bidder. In 1852 it even tried to dispossess diggers of their rights to the tiny areas to which their gold licences entitled them, by seeking to grant mining leases to large companies in already worked over areas. The Port Phillip Gold Mining Company was granted such a lease in 1853 at Fryer's Creek, but there was such an outcry from the 500 diggers who were still making good strikes there, that the company withdrew.

A related issue for many diggers was the fact that they were unrepresented in the Legislative Council of the new colony, although they were expected to pay taxes. Henry wrote a little on these subjects to his brother John in March 1853:

"The Legislative Council is constituted of 30 members, 10 of which are paid officials, 10 nominees appointed by La Trobe the Governor, and 10 Liberal members or independent members if you like the expression better, returned by the people in the respective electoral districts. This is a worse representation of the people than you have at home and as might be expected they don't always legislate according to the people's wish. Reform is wanted and reform must be granted soon or by and by the infant colony will get strong enough to declare independency."

"Another pique I have with the government is that they don't put up lands for sale in suitable quantities and lots sufficiently numerous to meet the demand. The consequence is that small plots of land suited to the small capitalist command an unnatural price. Squatting is a very lucrative and easy business for those who have two or three thousand pounds to begin with. These gentlemen have from 20.000 to perhaps 120,000 acres in their run and only pay £10 a year licence, in addition to 1d a head for sheep, 11/2d I think for cattle and 2d for horses. A mere acknowledgement."

Henry does not mention that the diggers did have at least one champion in John Pascoe Fawkner, who founded the Colonial Reform Association in November 1852. Its charter included winning the vote for working men and unlocking land for settlement. Fawkner was MP for the Kyneton district and used *Glassonby* as his headquarters when visiting the area. It would be interesting to think that Henry may have met him there. However, the franchise was not extended until 1855, after an event known as the Eureka Stockade, thereafter diggers became known as miners.

Elsewhere Henry suggests that the Butterworth family from Bolton Mill should consider bringing out a steam mill, as the streams would not be suitable for a water driven mill. He is insistent that blacksmith Joe Simpson would make a good living, especially if he could work alongside a wheelwright. He describes visiting a blacksmith called William Prince near Melbourne:

"He was very busy. Two or three horses were then standing for shoeing and he said the shoe he was then making was the 13th yesterday afternoon. They were all set on and he knew not how many more he should have before night. He had two men at work and said he wanted another two, one a wheelwright. He had several orders for new drays and unless he could get men he really could not fulfil them. Shoeing is £1 the set, other things in proportion, so tell Joseph Simpson that if he thinks of coming there is plenty of work and good pay. If he comes it would be well to try and get a wheelwright to join him. They do best together. If they had not money to establish business at first let them work as journeymen awhile and take care of their earnings."

Prices were so high because horses were worked all day every day for transport of everything, people and goods, and were so scarce that their owners could command high prices. This was another example of supply and demand economics.

However, Henry was not tempted to go on to a farm, although by this time he had a decent '*competency*' of £200 from his gold. He chose to go over to Van Diemen's Land, writing to his mother in March 1853: "*I had two or three motives in coming here. One was for a little recreation; another to see the place and ascertain how the prisoners were treated, who have been sent from England for their country's good, and third and last to trade a little in Van Demonian produce.*"

On the first point, he says the island is "*a beautiful place, diversified with hills and vallies, woods, rivers and plains and is a most salubrious climate. The Derwent is the finest river I ever saw and a splendid harbour at Hobart Town into which the largest vessel in the world might sail with ease, the river being 2 or 3 miles wide. "* The green hills rising to the peak of Mount Wellington which towers over the little harbour town, the blue of the river and the invigorating breezes blowing from the Southern Ocean must have been quite a tonic after the scorching dry conditions at the diggings during the mainland Summer. This Autumn weather reminded Henry of home most poignantly and he wrote six letters home between March and November that year.

Henry argues that it is not the fault of Van Diemen's Land that it is perceived to be a jail, "*.. it is not her fault. She must thank the virtuous and humane England for that. And though I never had any ambition to go to jail while at home, when I got out into Australia I confess I thought I should like to go to jail, of course not on the penetensiary but to see England's great prison and observe the treatment of the unfortunate inmates. Did I say unfortunates – there are some who have had the sentence of "hard labour" passed upon them "for the period of their natural life" who are now rolling in luxury, driving their carriage and have all that the heart could wish. Verily I believe they would have been more punished by being set at liberty at home where a man must work hard for all he gets.*"

The first penal colony to be established on the island, in 1822, was situated on the inhospitable west coast at Macquarie Harbour. Under an extremely harsh regime, the convicts were put to work cutting down trees in the rainforest. Some tried to escape, but few ever found their way to the relative civilization of Hobart Town across the unpathed mountains of the south west. Another penal settlement was established at Maria Island on the east of the island but both these were closed by 1833, when Governor Arthur established a settlement at

Port Arthur on the Tasman Peninsula in the south east. With the narrow neck of the peninsula guarded by fierce dogs and guards, this was considered escape-proof. Conditions for offenders became totally inhumane as some convicts were kept for weeks in solitary confinement in total darkness. A special chapel was built where convicts were seated in screened boxes so that they could see only the preacher. They could not communicate with anyone, even their guards. The idea was that where physical punishment had failed, the felon could be brought to redemption through silent contemplation of his sins.

When convict transportation to New South Wales ceased in 1840 those arriving in Van Diemens Land increased to a peak of 5,329 in 1842 and by 1848 it was the only destination for transportation in the British Empire. However, by this time there were many free settlers in Van Diemens Land, some of whom formed an Anti-Transportation League in 1850, which succeeded in its aim by 1853. Nevertheless, the reputation of Van Diemens Land was such that when the colony achieved self government in 1856 its name was changed to Tasmania.

By the time Henry arrived many of the 74,000 transported individuals had served out their sentences and settled peaceably in the colony. The system in place for some years previously was that arriving convicts would at first be put to work on government schemes well away from settled areas. They built a road between Hobart and Launceston and many public buildings. This probationary period varied according to the original crime and the behaviour of the individual. After that one could apply for a pass to work in private service. Many free settlers employed these men and women, giving them only board and lodging of the most minimal degree and sometimes treating them very harshly. However, continued good behaviour would result firstly in a ticket of leave, and ultimately an unconditional pardon. Thus a person who had committed a minor offence in England might eventually find himself with a steady living in the new country, at no expense to himself, except of course for enduring considerable hardship on a convict ship and separation from loved ones. Henry had talked to several men *"who wish they had been "legged" ten years sooner."* He still remained a little suspicious of ex-convicts, notwithstanding that *"The Missus of the Temperance Hotel at which I am lodging was sent out here as a convict and she is apparently a very decent old body, and a fellow lodger who is now sitting by the table upon which I write was a convict yet he is a very peacable and agreeable man."* Henry doesn't relate what crimes these people had committed, but many were transported for what we would consider very minor offences, such as stealing something to eat or even a handkerchief or two.

Henry enjoyed his spell of leisure in Hobart Town. He took advantage of the library at the Mechanics Institute - there were no fewer than nine libraries in this comparatively small town at the time. He attended the Scotch Free Church and the Scotch Established Church, and bought serious reading material from book auctions, where he was dismayed to find that popular novels and songs went for much more than Boswell's Life of Johnson and other worthy tomes.

In June 1853 he was still writing from Doyles Temperance Coffee House in Collins Street and there are some indications in two letters concerning the nature of the trade he was pursuing. He seems to have been buying up goods and produce needed at the diggings, as he quotes many prices to his father relating to the cost of transport up from Melbourne, explaining that *"The rainy season has set in and in consequence the bush roads are swampy and goods difficult of transit. A while ago goods might be conveyed up to the diggings from Melbourne for about £12 per ton. Now the price is from £70 to £80 per ton. A second cause of the present dullness of trade is the heavy arrivals of some kinds of merchandise from England and America."* This included wheat and oats. He also mentions that timber is bringing very high prices, and this may have influenced his subsequent enterprise, as one consignment he knew of "*cleared £11,000. Truly these are fortune making times for those who have the capital and spirit to embark in speculations of that nature.*"

He would like his father to send out good iron ploughs as "*They are a thing that will always bring a good price and will not be likely to be sent in quantities to glut the market. Good cart harness would also pay well.*" Interestingly, he also wants jam jars, "*If any of you come out bring 20 or 30 crates of jars likely to hold 3 or 4 lbs of jam each jar. I intend to make a few tons of jam next season.*" Whether he would do this while still lodging in Hobart is not clear, but the idea of jam making is not so strange, as Doran's Jam Factory, established in 1834 near Huonville, is now a tourist attraction.

Trading took Henry out of Hobart and into the interior of the island. He describes to his mother a particularly rough journey to a place 35 miles from Hobart, when he was grateful to a family called Weeding who farmed near Greenponds.
"*One gloomy morning I mounted the coach at 6 o'clock to go into their neighbourhood. We had not travelled far when the rain began to fall very heavily and I felt the difference of a stage coach to a railway carriage in the exposure to the inclemency of the weather. When we arrived at Greenponds I had about 4 or 5 miles to travel over the steep hills and through rough and long grass and what rendered the case worse I nearly lost the heel of one of my boots. However, on arriving at the Hunting Ground Mrs Weeding gave me a hearty welcome though I could by no means be a pleasant guest.*"

(James and John Weeding emigrated from Surrey to Hobart in 1823, arriving with a large fortune and a letter of introduction to the Lieutenant Governor. This enabled them to acquire a grant of 1000 acres of land near Macquarie Springs. However, they were continually harassed by so called bush rangers and after nine years they moved close to the new town of Oatlands in the Lower Midlands. In 1839 John Weeding purchased a further 1000 acres at a place called the Hunting Ground, situated in the Jordan valley in an area known as Green Ponds. His home was called 'Sunnyside' and there is a mountain in the area called 'Mt Weeding'.)

As Henry had little spare clothing, these kind people lent him dry clothes and he stayed in the area for nearly a fortnight. This he gave as an example to his mother that he was not friendless in a foreign land, as she feared. Among other deals struck in this area, he *"closed a bargain with Mr Weeding for 300 bushels of oats to be delivered as soon as they could be dressed up, a few of them being then to thrash."* However, before the deal could go through, the price of oats fell, which would have meant a loss to Henry, but Mr Weeding insisted on keeping back some of the grain for seed, and Henry gave this as an example of the good honest people he was mixing with.

During this venture Henry Richardson seems to have been living in Melbourne, so that he was on hand to receive the consignments of produce which Henry was despatching from Hobart. It may seem strange that the colony of Victoria was so dependent on what we now regard as the rather minor state of Tasmania. However, the island had been a colony since the early 1800s and was extensively settled from that time. Large areas of forest had been cleared, some by convict labour, so that extensive runs were created for cattle and sheep rearing, and there were fertile river valleys, such as that of the Jordan mentioned above, suited to grain and fruit production. With the expanding population of Victoria owing to the gold rush, Van Dieman's Land farmers were in a good position to capitalize on their goods, although this was short lived owing to the imports coming from America and Europe.

Tragedy on the Huon

By September 1853 Henry was writing from Flights Bay on the Huon River, though he may have gone there about a month earlier. This river rises high in the Hartz Mountains and flows eastwards until it takes a sharp turn to the south, emerging into the sea via a long estuary with many tributaries, which is roughly parallel to the Derwent estuary at the head of which lies Hobart. Owing to the dense forests which reached right to the water's edge, the Huon was initially explored only by boat. Early settlers were usually aided by convict labour to fell trees, but converting the cleared land for agriculture was a backbreaking task. By the 1850s an overland route had been prospected, but it was still only a track, impassable by wheeled vehicles for much of its length, because of tree stumps, swamps and river crossings served only by canoe or fallen tree trunks.

One of the indigenous trees was called the Huon pine, a softwood tree which takes 500 years to mature and can live for 2500 years. Its yellow coloured wood is highly resinous and resistant to water and therefore valuable for ship building and house building purposes. Little wonder, then, that this was viewed as a very valuable resource, and the timber trade from the Huon was well established by 1829 when 200 tonnes were exported to London. Most timber, however, was for the home market in Hobart and on the mainland, until in 1849 gold was discovered in California. Sales to the USA which were practically non-existent in 1848, went from £5,958 in 1849 to £12, 949 in 1850. This market had declined by 1851, but the discovery of gold in Victoria in that year stimulated a renewed demand for timber products. The price of shingles, used for roofing, went from 7 shillings per thousand in 1851 to 30 shillings in March 1853 up to a peak of 50-60 shillings in August.

Lithograph *The Gum Forest* by Rbt. Elwes, 1854, courtesy of
Allport Library and Museum of Fine Arts, State Library of Tasmania

Many settlements grew up along the river's edge, one of which
was known as Flight's Bay, though its name was later changed

to Waterloo. It is on the west bank of the river, approximately 38 miles overland from Hobart. Later, when much of the land was bought up by a man called Bolton Stafford Bird, the name was changed to Waterloo. This is said to be because he had a hard battle to clear the land and it was overlooked by Mount Wellington. There is a family named Bird in present day Bolton, but it is not known whether there is any connection with Tasmania.

On September 11th Henry wrote to his mother:

"*Mr Richardson and I are at present living in a hut on the banks of the River Huon at Flights Bay where the river may be said to merge into an arm of the sea for vessels of almost any tonnage might with perfect safety come up thus far, in full sail. This morning the reflected beams of the sun make a part of this bay appear like a sheet of glass. Another part has a gentle curl playing up it with the morning breeze. Here and there its surface as a mirror reflects the clouds and the surrounding woodland hills. This as you are aware, is a Winter's morning, yet all around is clad in green. The bushwood assumes a thousand different forms. Some of the shrubs would grace a gentleman's pleasure ground, but although they are strowed about in apparent confusion, yet to me they have a charm of which they would be deprived were they placed in that artificial capacity. They have here all that luxuriousness with which a bounteous Nature can adorn them. The other day Nature seemed convulsed – one squall of wind after another howled through the forest, the Bay was all emotion, the rain fell in torrents and the peals of distant thunder were frequent. Now all is calm, serene and beautiful, and the little birds, though they cannot sing like the thrush, the linnet or the nightingale are manifesting their joy in the best and sweetest strains with which Nature has endowed them.*" He describes the tall trees "whose aspiring trunks *shoot up to a height seldom thought of and more seldom realised in England.*"

It is not clear how Henry and Mr Richardson got into the timber trade. Unless they were working for someone else, they would have had to purchase a timber felling licence. Maybe this is what they did, as Henry wrote to his sister of "*our intention of laying out our capital in timber, shipping it to Melbourne and in the meantime working with our hands. We have mounted the saw horse and are whipping along having nearly overcome all the difficulties of learners.* " There must have been many men tempted by the money to be made from timber, as Henry mentions that there is no longer any public worship at Flights Bay as "*the minister has resigned his appointment which only brought him in £200 per annum and has a steam saw mill which will at present clear nearly £100 a week.*"

He is referring to the Reverend Mr Andrewartha, officially Missionary Chaplain for the Huon District since the mid-1840s. In 1850 he purchased 600 acres at Flights Bay and in 1852 with another clergyman as partner he established a steam-powered sawmill there. However a very public dispute erupted between the two, which resulted in a court case and Andrewartha's resignation of his chaplaincy position. This grasping attitude to money by a man of God was certainly not to Henry's taste.

"*He still continues to preach when at home which is not more than every alternate Sunday. I still think that many ministers only make a convenience of their religious profession. They display devotion's every grace except that rather important item, the heart – that they fix on the gain in the shape of hard cash which the other display is the means of grasping. Mr Richardson and I attend services when held. When there is none we pass our Sundays in reading or examining the works of Nature and contrasting their order and regularity with the discrepancies, follies and irregularities of man, not forgetting our own.*"

However, in late November the tide had turned, Henry reporting that "*we have had a great decline in the timber trade – prices* at a slump about a third of what they were 4 months ago. We are thankful we have entered no further into it than we have. We at one time contemplated making arrangements to carry on the business on a rather extensive scale. Much better that we did not."

He remains philosophical, however, arguing that "When I'm not making much money I'm gaining experience and experience is in many cases better than gold. I have not the least doubt but I can make an independency in a few years if I have a continuation of good health."

His health at this point was extremely good, as he pointed out that he weighed more – at just less than 14 stones – than he did in England, and was able to walk the 38 miles to Hobart in one day, when spurred on by the prospect of "good news from a far country".

In the only surviving letter to his sister, Henry reveals more of his feelings than he generally does to his father and mother. She has given him news of the state of farming in England, which she says is looking up in general, and he asks how his young brother Billy is getting along with his horse named 'Bonny'. "I suppose he will be doing his furrows straight, or if not telling Bonny to look what bad work she is making."

This leads him to imagine the household scene and his feelings for the family:
"I often think of you all and picture you out in my mind after the toils of the day are over, surrounding the fire in the old house at home, conning over the business of the day and now and then perchance dropping a word on the one that is not, for I find by your letters I'm not forgotten. Though thousands of miles lie between us and two thousand waves dash and foam themselves, rearing their mighty heads as in defiance of our reunion as a whole family, yet in mind we may partake of that bliss which is reserved for the higher powers of our nature. We may experience feelings of love and sympathy which might

never have been called into exercise had not a separation of body taken place. Indeed I feel that it is the case. While at home I never thought that I loved my parents, my sister and brothers with a tithe of that ardour which I've experienced since I felt my lips pressed with the parting kiss."

He has no regrets about leaving home, however.

"I certainly am no advocate for young men, especially after they reach years of maturity, hanging over their parents and depending on them. Such a course is, I think, calculated to do no good to either parents or sons and may do much harm because men don't all see alike and if they have got a will of their own (and every man ought to have) there will in all probability arise little bits of unpleasant dissentions. I think that every person after arriving at years of maturity ought to think and act for himself without restraint, save in the shape of advice. My views on these points may be faulty, but I cannot help thinking they are reasonable and right. Were my parents in need, which thank God they are not, I could give them anything to the last farthing I possessed; were they ill I should do all in my power for their recovery, but that "do this or that in this or that way" I abhor, and perhaps the manifestations of that dislike will be among the most bitter recollections I have left at home. ... I am thankful, dear sister, that I have a home – a good home at Bolton – because I feel that you are all dear to my heart, and have a place in my warmest affections, but it is not a home to come back to. It may, and I trust it will be a home to visit – I would this moment cheerfully give £50 to spend a week with you, but money would not entice me into my former sphere. After these expressions you will perceive I am not the man to beat a retreat because I may meet with a few difficulties. I have very little sympathy for young people who are continually finding lions in the way and starting back at any little thing that may be unpleasant. For my part I can do with a few difficulties if there is a prospect of a better time coming, but the needless *and heart sickening drudgery of a farm that would scarcely afford the rent I never could bear to think of."*

The last letter to his mother, written on November 26th 1853 is very brief, mostly an acknowledgement of one from her dated July 9th which he had only just received. He is sorry to hear her health is bad and thanks her for sending out local papers. He explains that the timber trade is now not doing so well, but he is not disheartened. He finishes by saying that "*I should have been highly gratified if father had written me. Give my best love to him and tell him that I try to interpet his silence the best way I can. Your affectionate son, Henry.*"

There was a long dry spell of weather in the Summer of 1853-4 and bush fires erupted, mostly on the eastern side of the river, during December. A great deal of property was lost but no lives. On January 11th, however, new fires broke out, fanned by strong winds, and areas on both sides of the river were affected this time. One eyewitness stated that the flames "*swept along with such fearful rapidity that the most experienced bushmen had the greatest difficulty in escaping with their lives ... the heat was so intense that it was difficult to breathe.*"

The *Hobart Town Advertiser* of January 14th reported that "*It appears that a short time before 12 o'clock nothing was to be observed beyond a few light puffs of smoke rising here and there in the bush; at half past 12 o'clock the whole district appeared to be in a blaze. The fiery torrent came roaring down with the velocity of an avelanch, cutting off almost the possibility of escape. The crashing of the falling timber; the roaring of the fire; mingled at all times with wild shrieks of agony and despair, are described to have been truly awful.*"

Henry Richardson's letter, dated Melbourne February 6th 1854, describes Henry Dent's actions on that same Wednesday at Flights Bay.

"*The day was begun by his reading one or two chapters in the Bible, as we each did on alternate mornings. He was deeply impressed with the importance of spiritual things. Everything passed on during the forenoon – the 11th of January with the best good humour. I never saw him in better spirits. At 1 o'clock, the day being warm with a hot wind, we had been bathing in the bay. We then had dinner. About 3 o'clock we commenced to saw. In about 10 minutes after this the wind began to blow a complete hurricane. The fire had been burning on the ranges for a day or two. It now began to approach us with the most alarming rapidity; so soon as we became conscious of our danger we threw a few pieces of timber from the pit which was likely to ignite, and ran into the hut, having thrown out a few articles, the whole of which did not occupy more than two or three minutes. He told me to run with the bedding to the beach and try to save it. I immediately did as required and in less than half a minute deposited it there. I then attempted to return, as he had not followed me as I expected, but found it impossible to do so as the fire was already across the path by which I had come. So soon as I durst venture for the fire and smoke, though still at imminent danger from falling trees and branches, I did so, when I was horror struck to find him lying in the middle of a cart road, not having got more than 50 yards from the hut. He must have been choked by the smoke. The smoke from the underwood which is green and full of gas is so strong that anyone breathing it is almost immediately suffocated.*"

Henry's body was taken to the town of Franklin, about 12 miles away, for an inquest and burial. The page recording his death states as cause of death '*Burnt to death by Bush Fire*' and there are five similar entries on the same page, two other '*Labourers*', one '*Labourer's wife*' and two children. Many other settlers were caught up in the tragedy, 32 out of 34 huts in the area being destroyed, as well as the saw mill belonging to the Reverend Andrewartha and other buildings on the water's edge.

Henry Richardson explained that he and Henry had lost everything except 25,000 feet of timber which was already on the beach. Ironically, this was loaded up and shipped to Geelong the very next week, on the same vessel by which the partners had intended to leave Van Dieman's Land. Henry Richardson then travelled via Hobart to Melbourne where he sought to wind up their affairs. In a subsequent letter he set out in detail the terms of their partnership and the money due to Henry's estate, and then asked that his parents let him keep it for two or three years as a loan on which he would pay 8% interest, as he had set up a store at Kyneton, and hoped they would regard it as an investment. However, of a store owned by a Richardson in Kyneton there seems to be no trace.

It would have been June or July 1854 before news of this terrible disaster reached Bolton. How would parents feel to know that for the last six months when they thought that their son was happy and prospering in the new country, he had in fact been dead and buried? What to do, how to tell your friends and neighbours? How to remember your firstborn son? At some point the Dents caused a memorial stone to be erected in the churchyard, so that there was at least a place where his memory could be honoured. A hundred and fifty years later its intriguing inscription and the careful preservation of Henry's letters has led to the retelling of his fascinating story.

The memorial stone to Henry Dent in Bolton churchyard

Postscript

The Palmers of Kyneton

Henry mentions the Palmers many times, and they were very helpful to him and Henry Richardson and many other immigrants on their way to and from the goldfields of Mount Alexander. As they seemed to be a prominent family, I have researched a little of their history with the help of Kyneton Historical Society Inc.

John Palmer was born in May 1793 in the Parish of Addingham, Cumberland and married the 21 year old Ellen Shearman of Orton, Westmoreland in her home village in 1822. They had 13 children of whom 10 lived to adulthood. As the first five were born in Orton, it can be assumed that John was working in that area. After 1832 the children's birthplace is Glassonby, which is in the parish of Addingham, so presumably he returned to his father's farm at that time. In 1848 with the youngest child only a few months' old, the family set sail for Australia. They may have taken advantage of the assisted passage scheme, which favoured families with large numbers of children, who would soon be able to work in the new colony. The Palmers' eldest boys were already in their late teens, so would be able to earn wages as soon as they landed. Henry Dent's letter mentions two Shearmans at the diggings, who may have been Ellen's brothers, and an old gentleman named Shearman who was probably her father.

In 1850 John Palmer was one of the first settlers to purchase at auction 200 acres of Crown Land at Kyneton. He set about building a substantial two storey house of bluestone with a pitched roof and cellar which was completed in 1852. He called it Glassonby after his birthplace, and it remained in family ownership until it was demolished to make way for a road.

Henry Dent mentions that Mr Palmer's sons Robert, John and William were at the diggings at the same time as himself and Henry Richardson, so their gold discoveries no doubt added to the prosperity which was being achieved by the farm, where dairy cattle were kept and grain grown. The position near the road between Melbourne and Mt Alexander was particularly favourable for such an enterprise and the family became prominent citizens of the area, such that J.P Fawkner MP made Glassonby his headquarters when in the district. John Palmer died in 1866 and Ellen in 1885. Their youngest son Joseph, aged only 4 when he arrived in Australia, went on to become a solicitor and his son a doctor, so the move to Australia had certainly been very successful.

A fragment of a letter written by John Palmer is reproduced in a book called *The Gold Finder of Australia* by John Sherer. There is no indication as to whom it was written or the date, but I have a strong feeling that it may have been addressed to a member of the Dent family and that it may have been one of the reasons why Henry Dent and Henry Richardson decided to emigrate. It was probably written in 1851 as he mentions that '*I am about to send to England a quantity of gold to the amount of £700 to get coined into sovereigns. Four of my sons obtained this in six weeks at Mount Alexander*' and the first gold discoveries were only made in that year.

He also says that
'*I have now 200 acres of good land ... I must tell you that a dairy is a good thing here. I milk fourteen cows at present, and I intend to increase the number to twenty or thirty. We sell all our butter at 2s per lb, and I have had 1s 3d per lb bid for*

all the cheese I have; but I have refused it, as I can get a good deal more. I know you people in England will dispute this, but I write the truth. I am living fifty five miles from Melbourne, one mile from Kyneton, a town of ten months standing, with a population of 400 inhabitants. The military road to Melbourne comes close past my house, so, you see, I have an opportunity of seeing all the traffic to and from the mines. In comparison the roads day by day are thronged the same as one of yours on market day.'

Like many letter writers of the time, he urges other English farming families to come out to Australia.
'I can truly say that this is the best country under the sun for the industrious labourer. It is a pity that there is not thousands of such here, as there is plenty of employment and good wages. This is the land where no-one need repent coming to. Everyone may do well if they try, and are steady, I don't mean to say that everyone without exception will get riches, but their industry will be well rewarded. I often do say, it is such a pity that so many are starving in England.'

Later in the letter he writes:
' I remember you once saying to me, near Long Meg, that you would never go out to any colony to get riches, as you would be sure to be disappointed. My answer was, neither would I, but I think it will be better for my family. I never, however, thought of getting gold in pound weights. I have much reason to praise and be thankful to God for providentially moving me and my family to come to this land of plenty.'

The reference to Long Meg, a group of standing stones not far from the river Eden and Glassonby village again poses the question: was this letter addressed to John or Henry Dent, who could have known John Palmer through the Methodist church circuit?

Furthermore, he writes:

'I always respect and remember you with gratitude ever since you set shoulder to me as my friend and G___ and yourself, I acknowledge, were friends indeed.'

There is an allusion in one of Henry Dent's letters to his father that Mr Palmer refuses to accept payment for services rendered to him, because of a debt he owes to his father.

There is definitely a connection in religious sentiment between John Palmer and the person to whom he is writing, as he assures him that *'there are all sorts of religious societies here, the same as in England.'*

Finally, there is the tantalising remark:

'I promised H.R.... a letter, but I have not done so. Let him see this, and any one else you think proper.'

Could this HR be Henry Richardson, schoolmaster of Cliburn, whose son, another Henry, was Henry Dent's companion to Australia?

The Richardsons

When Henry Dent died, Henry Richardson wrote to his parents to tell them the sad news, and later he told them that he was at Kyneton where he had set up a store. As yet I have found no record of such a business, but in a report on farming in the Kyneton district in 1864, directly after a paragraph relating to the Palmer's farm called Glassonby, I came across the following:

'*Very near to Glassonby is Willow Bank (80 acres) a farm belonging to Mr Joseph Richardson, who has another of 200 acres a few miles away.*'

Henry had a brother called Joseph, who would have been 29 years of age in 1864. Could it be that Henry managed to persuade at least one of his three brothers to go out to join him? On the 1851 census Joseph, aged 16, was listed as a farm labourer, so it's possible that in the ten or twelve intervening years he had earned enough to buy the land for this farm, maybe with his elder brother's help.

Such speculations are perhaps idle, but it's fascinating to conjure up the lives of these enterprising people who travelled 15,000 miles to make a new life for themselves and their descendants.

Thanks to

Barbara Cotton, author of *Changing Times: The Millenium Story of the People of Bolton, Westmorland,* Hayloft 2001, who asked me to write about Henry Dent for a Flower Festival at All Saints Church, Bolton, and lent me the letters which formed the basis of my book. Also for allowing use of photos from the unofficial village archive of which she is the custodian.

William Henry Dent Robinson, great nephew of Henry Dent, who sent the collection of letters and Henry's photograph to Barbara Cotton and later encouraged me in writing this account.

Max Robinson, brother of William, who many years ago typed out the handwritten letters, thus ensuring their survival in legible form.

Margery Brown, great great niece of Henry Dent, for allowing me to words and writing from Henry's poetry book.

Kyneton Historical Society Inc for recommending
Nothing but Gold, the Diggers of 1852, by Robyn Annear, publ by Text Publishing, Melbourne 1999 and helping me in my researches of the Mt Alexander goldfields, the Palmer family etc.
Reminiscences of Fryerstown by G O Brown, printed by Castlemain Mail, 1983

Huon Valley Council for their informative book *A History of the Huon and the Far South, Vol 1: Before the Orchards Grew,* by Richie Woolley and Wayne Smith, publ 2004

Also used for Background Material

Life and Death in the Age of Sail: The passage to Australia by Robin Haines, publ. by the National Maritime Museum, London 2003

Sailing to Australia: Shipboard Diaries by Nineteenth Century British Emigrants, by Andrew Hassam, publ by Manchester University Press, 1994

Acknowledgements

The National Library of Australia for permission to reproduce the lithograph *Fryers Creek, Mount Alexander diggings*, by Samuel Thomas Gill 1818-1880, publ. Melbourne: Macartney & Galbraith, 1852 (nla.pic-an 7537718) on p. 42

The State Library of Tasmania, Allport Library & Museum of Fine Arts, Tasmanian Archive and Heritage Office for permission to reproduce *A sawyer's Hut on the River Huon* by Wm knight 1842 on p. V, and the lithograph, *Gum Forest,* by Robert Elwes, publ. London: Hurst & Blackett 1854 on p. 63

Lightning Source UK Ltd.
Milton Keynes UK
20 December 2010

164659UK00002B/20/P